Taubes' Guide to Oil Painting
by Frederic Taubes

Reinhold Publishing Corporation
New York

Copyright, 1965
Reinhold Publishing Corporation
All rights reserved
Printed in the United States of America
Library of Congress Catalog Card Number 65-24060
Published by Reinhold Publishing Corporation
430 Park Avenue, New York, N.Y.

Designed by Charles N. Smith
Type set by Lettick Typografic, Inc.
Printed by The Comet Press, Inc.
Bound by Publishers Book Bindery, Inc.

Other Books by Frederic Taubes

Painting Techniques, Ancient and Modern, Viking Press, Inc.

The Quickest Way To Paint Well, Viking Press, Inc.

The Quickest Way To Draw Well, Viking Press, Inc.

Better Frames for your Pictures, Viking Press, Inc.

The Mastery of Oil Painting, Viking Press, Inc.

Pictorial Anatomy of the Human Body, Viking Press, Inc.

The Technique of Oil Painting, Dodd, Mead & Company

You Don't Know What You Like, Dodd, Mead & Company

Studio Secrets, Watson-Guptill Publications

Oil Painting for the Beginner, Watson-Guptill Publications

The Amateur Painter's Handbook, Dodd, Mead & Company

The Painter's Question and Answer Book, Watson-Guptill Publications

Anatomy of Genius, Dodd, Mead & Company

Pictorial Composition and the Art of Drawing, Dodd, Mead & Company

Taubes' Paintings and Essays of Art, Dodd, Mead & Company

New Essays on Art, Watson-Guptill Publications

Oil Painting and Tempera, Watson-Guptill Publications

Pen and Ink Drawing, Watson-Guptill Publications

The Art and Technique of Portrait Painting, Dodd, Mead & Company

Modern Art Sweet and Sour, Watson-Guptill Publications

The Art and Technique of Landscape Painting, Watson-Guptill Publications

New Techniques in Painting, Dodd, Mead & Company

Abracadabra and Modern Art, Dodd, Mead & Company

Contents

Color Illustrations

Suggested Equipment for Beginners

Easel
Set of round sable brushes
Bristle brushes Numbers 4, 5, 7, 8, 10
Painting Knives
Canvas made of cotton. 12 by 16 inches and 16 by 20 inches
Stretchers in sizes corresponding to canvas
Stretcher Keys
Masonite panels up to 12 by 16 inches
Restricted list of colors
Painting media and varnishes
Miscellaneous materials
  Turpentine
  Charcoal
  Fixative
  Tracing paper
  Thumbtacks
  Upholstery nails
  Gesso priming

Part 1 gives detailed descriptions of the materials listed above.

Introduction

Three decades of teaching have convinced me that there is no possible substitute for habits of good craftsmanship established at the very outset of any effort in the art of painting. This applies not only to those who turn to art as a profession but also to the increasingly large group of people who take up painting as an avocation, for the sheer joy of expressing their inner sensibilities in the wonderfully satisfying activity of painting a picture.

By now the total number of students I have taught must be many thousands; and judging by results, my teaching methods have been remarkably successful. Therefore in this book, prepared essentially to meet the special needs of beginners, I have followed my established teaching plan, stressing the importance of a thorough grounding in sound technique as the first step for anyone who wants to paint. The methods recommended here will also help experienced painters improve their technique.

Technique is the painter's alphabet—the means by which he can translate his vision into visible form. To attain good technique, the painter must become completely familiar with the tools of his craft, and with their uses. What are painter's tools? They are the lowly brush and the painting knife. Certain artistic effects can be best achieved by one tool, and others by another tool; the nature of these tools must be well understood if the artist wishes to take command of his means of expression. The same imperative applies to the colors, their properties, actions, and interactions; to the vehicles and the media that are the lifeblood of these colors; to the supports upon which a painting is done, and to the many other operations and practices in the creation of a work of art. All of these things add up to what we mean by technique.

Most of the successful techniques used today were developed through the ages by great painters whose works are immortal. All the instructions condensed into this small book are based on the teachings of these great masters of the past—in truth, these masters could be considered the de facto authors.

Currently some art cliques, fortunately diminishing in influence, continue to promote the fallacy that present-day artists should ignore the entire artistic heritage of our civilization and start painting simply by intuition. I do not believe that any worthwhile work of art, however modest, can be created by such an uninformed approach, for then the artist quite literally does not know what he is doing or why—he just hopes that somehow what he has put down will turn out to be a great picture.

There is a large body of literature on the subject of painting technique but much of it lacks any real authority. In these matters I have never accepted the word of others. Instead, for many years I have conducted my own research and experiments, often in consultation with trained and highly qualified specialists including world-famous museum conservators here and abroad. The only materials and techniques I use and recommend are those that I have tested myself, patiently, over long periods of time.

While several of my previous books contain various results of my research, the present volume contains the essence of all the basic knowledge, distilled and brought up to date. I have written it for those who want to follow a sound time-tested system that will develop the a-b-c skills necessary for proficiency, ease, and true satisfaction in the art of painting.

Frederic Taubes
1965

Part 1.

Basic Tools and Materials

It goes without saying, of course, that anyone who wants to paint must first gain an understanding of the painter's tools and materials, and their uses. A familiarity with these requisites must be established before starting to paint, for their nature and character will inevitably influence the painter's work, as I pointed out in my introduction. Part 1 will be devoted to this purpose.

Chapter 1.

Brushes and Painting Knives

Sable Brushes

Five basic round sable brushes with short handles of equal thickness should be part of every painter's equipment (Fig. 1). These brushes should be handled much like writing tools; the small ones are used specifically for delineation. Long-handled brushes are a handicap; the extra length extending beyond one's hand acts as a counter-balance that nudges the sable hair away from the canvas. Thin handles, such as those found on watercolor brushes, are also undesirable for the oil painter because they do not rest well in a hand that is unaccustomed to working with a flimsy holder.

The smallest brush shown, Number 1, permits precise strokes, such as those needed for fine details on a portrait, for example. Numbers 2 and 3 are similar brushes in large dimensions. They are also suitable for detail work, as well as for forceful strokes on broad surfaces.

Number 4, known as a script liner, is indispensable in still life painting, in landscape painting, and in all painting situations that call for great freedom of execution. This brush can follow the most delicate impulses of one's fingers. The long, thin body of its hair takes on a large quantity of paint. Therefore it can operate on a canvas for a long time without interruption for reloading. This, in turn, allows the initial impulse of the painter's hand to develop with unimpeded freedom and spontaneity.

The last brush, Number 5, called a striper, permits even greater freedom. In contrast to the script liner, the terminal point of this brush is chisel-shaped. This characteristic forces a more vigorous application of paint.

Delineations made with these sable brushes are demonstrated in Figs. 5A and 5B, page 30.

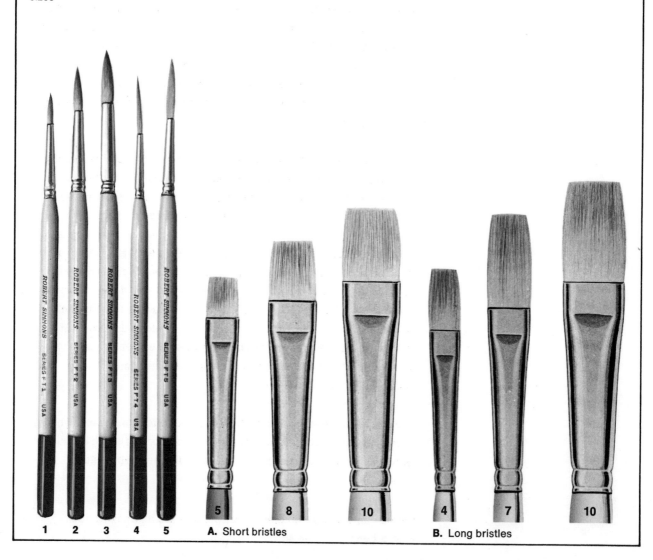

Figure 1.
Round sable brushes with short, balanced, uniformly thick handles

Figure 2.
Bristle brushes in useful sizes

ROBERT SIMMONS SERIES FT 1 USA
ROBERT SIMMONS SERIES FT 2 USA
ROBERT SIMMONS SERIES FT 3 USA
ROBERT SIMMONS SERIES FT 4 USA
ROBERT SIMMONS SERIES FT 5 USA

1   2   3   4   5

5   8   10

4   7   10

A. Short bristles

B. Long bristles

Bristle Brushes

Six bristle brushes are required (Figs. 2A and 2B). Those shown in Fig. 2A have short bristles suitable for forceful applications of paint, as in underpainting, for example. Their most useful sizes are Numbers 5, 8, and 10.

Brushes with longer bristles have greater elasticity. They are used for more fluent, delicate work, and for blending of colors. Sizes 4, 7, and 10 are best (Fig. 2B). These are particularly useful for work on small and medium-sized canvases. Characteristic markings made by bristle brushes are demonstrated in Fig. 6, page 32.

For work on a very small scale, or for the extremely delicate blending of colors occasionally called for, flat sable brushes $1/8$ to $3/4$ inches wide may be used. It must be stressed, however, that the nature of the paint diluent used in our work is such that fusion of the paint can be achieved even with a bristle brush. However, if linseed oil is used for thinning paint, or, still worse, if linseed oil and turpentine—the favorite medium of those unfamiliar with painting techniques—are used, such a fusion or blending cannot be easily and efficiently done with bristle brushes.

Cleaning Brushes

The best way to remove moist paint is with soap and water. Slightly hardened paint should be softened with turpentine or "painters' thinner," a solvent available in every hardware store. Very dry paint can be removed only by soaking the brush in a standard paint remover, such as Red Devil. Such commercial paint removers, contrary to common belief, are not harmful to sable hair or to bristles. After the paint has softened, wash the brush with soap and water, being very careful to clean every particle of paint from the neck of the ferrule, where decay starts. After the round sable brushes have been washed, they should be brought to a fine point between one's lips and allowed to dry. Otherwise, as the brush dries, the sable hair will spread and separate. To keep bristle brushes in shape, wrap a piece of soft paper, such as newsprint, around the bristles while they are still wet.

Figure 3.
Three painting knives in
basic shapes

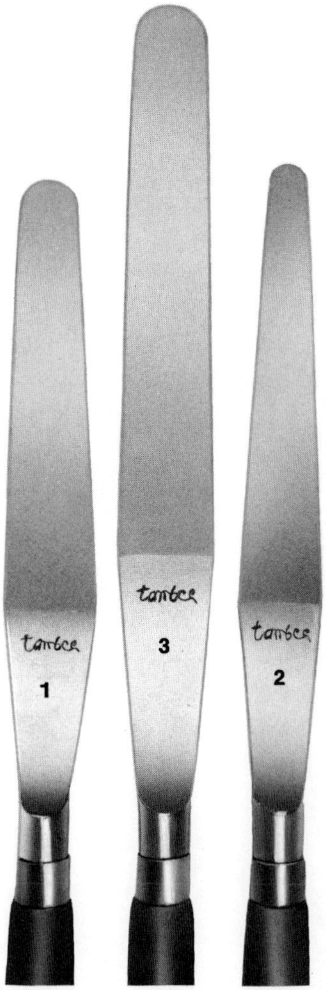

Painting Knives

These tools are of great importance; often a major part of a painting will require their use. Three knives, each one with different properties, are necessary (Fig. 3). The first knife pictured, Number 1, is designed for underpainting. It is made with a firmer blade than the other two knives so that the stiff, undiluted paint used for underpainting can be applied vigorously enough to fill the interstices of the canvas. The middle knife, Number 3, is a delicate instrument with a tapering, elastic blade that responds readily to the dictates of the artist's fingers. It is suitable for both detail work and for applying paint in broad areas. The last knife, Number 2, is usually called a blender. Large surfaces of paint can be blended and smoothed with this knife; it is useful not only for such work as finishing the underpainting of large surfaces, but also in finishing the painting itself.

Painting knives are used chiefly for work on canvas. They do not operate well on panels, because a rigid surface does not respond sufficiently to the impact of the blade.

Taking care of Knives

First of all, the blades must always be kept immaculately clean, otherwise they will mar the painting surface. The blades are not subject to rust, however, even when not in use. They are protected by an infinitesimal coating of protective oil that always remains on the metallic surface after all the paint has been cleaned off the blade. But painting knives do have a characteristic that needs careful watching—through frequent use, the blades may develop edges sharp enough to endanger not only fingers, but the canvas as well. If this happens, the sharp edges should be dulled. To do this, hold the knife upright against a piece of carborundum paper and rotate the edges. During this process, a burr will form on both sides of the blade. This burr should be sanded off with carborundum paper.

Figure 4.
Keys used to wedge the
stretcher bars apart

Chapter 2.

Canvas, Panels, and Miscellaneous Equipment

The Canvas

Canvas is made of either cotton or linen fiber. The first is considerably cheaper than the second, but it is not necessarily inferior. Both come in various grains.

Choosing the proper canvas is important. The surface quality should be the first consideration, for this quality can radically affect the painter's work. The right grain for the task at hand can often make his work easy. The wrong grain often impedes its progress.

Unduly coarse-grained canvas, will make it difficult to create a paint surface on which brush or knife strokes register easily. Coarse grain needs a great deal of paint to fill its interstices, and even if paint is heavily applied, it will swallow up brush or knife marks.

Generally speaking, the smoother the canvas surface, the more easily brush marks will assert themselves. On the other hand, a surface that is too smooth tends to make the paint slide and slither. Canvas surfaces without definite "tooth," or grain, are not satisfactory for work with the painting knife. Such canvas is primarily for alla prima painting, described on page 55.

All in all, a medium-smooth canvas, double-primed, is the best choice for beginners. "Double-primed" means that the raw fabric has been treated with two layers of priming solution. Canvas can be purchased by the yard. This costs much less than buying it already stretched. Stretching canvas is a very simple process even for the inexperienced. Stretcher bars and wooden keys can be bought in any art supply store.

Stretching Canvas

1. Assemble four stretcher bars to form a rectangular frame.
2. Fold the canvas over one of the stretcher bars. Anchor it with a $3/8$ inch upholstery tack hammered through the center. A stapler can be used for this purpose.
3. Pull the folded canvas horizontally toward one end of the bar. Anchor it with a tack. Follow the same procedure at the other end.
4. Fasten the canvas firmly with tacks placed about two inches apart along the entire bar.
5. Follow this procedure along the opposite stretcher bar, and at the same time pull the canvas taut vertically.
6. Fasten the canvas along the two remaining stretcher bars, using the same method. While tacking the last bar, stretch the canvas taut.
7. Nail down the folds that form at the corners.
8. Place the wooden keys in the slots provided for them at the corners of the stretchers, Fig. 4. Hammer in gently. This will pry the bars apart and thus correct slack, making even the limpest canvas taut as a drum.

The Panel

The best panel for our purpose is Masonite, available at any lumber yard. Sizes up to about 20 to 24 inches, $1/8$ inch thick, will not need supporting braces. Larger panels warp easily, hence they may require cross-bar bracing, unless a panel $1/4$ inch thick is used. However, such panels are rather heavy.

Ready-prepared Masonite panels are available in most supply stores. But in my experience these are all unsatisfactory in one respect or another. Some are too absorbent to be used for oil painting. And the surfaces of all commercial panels are much too smooth, due to the fact that the gesso surface is sprayed on and often smoothed after the spraying. This gives the panels a mechanical finish that imparts a certain slickness to the painting.

However, with the availability of a new acrylic material called Liquitex Gesso, priming a Masonite panel has become a simple and effortless operation. Before priming, the gesso should be thinned with an equal amount of water. Using a broad brush, the mixture should be applied thinly to both sides of the panel in order to prevent warping. The priming dries in a few minutes. Then a second and third coat should be applied. A surface prepared in this way can be used for oil painting as soon as it is dry, that is, within minutes. Thinning the somewhat thick gesso solution with water is necessary to avoid brush marks. Experience has proven that heavy brush marks on the priming will always interfere with the texture of paint applied over it. For alla prima work, only the smooth side of the panel is suitable.

Miscellaneous Equipment
So far we have dealt only with the tools and supports used in painting. There are other requisites. A palette and, of course, an oil cup are essential. The palette should have a surface measuring at least 12 by 16 inches. Preferably, it should be made of wood. I consider wood the most agreeable material for this purpose.

An easel is required. The nature of the easel depends entirely on the purchase price. However, students should know that inexpensive easels, if they are sturdy enough, can be serviceable and satisfactory.

Another indispensable item is vine charcoal for sketching preliminary to painting. I state specifically "vine" charcoal because its marks can be wiped out easily with a rag. Carbon charcoal in stick or in pencil form is not suitable for this purpose. Fixative spray, sold in spray pressure cans, should be used to render charcoal marks indelible and so prevent smearing, which must be taken into account when painting over the preliminary drawing.

Thin, translucent sketching paper is needed for developing a composition —working directly on the canvas with charcoal can become a messy job, especially for complex designs that may call for many changes. Transfer paper is also needed. Use graphite paper not carbon paper for transferring a drawing to the canvas—tracings made with carbon paper will bleed through the dry paint film. If graphite paper is not available, an adequate transfer paper can be prepared by covering tracing paper with dense charcoal, or still better, with pastel marks.

Chapter 3.

Physical Properties of Paints
Diluents, Varnishes, and Drying Agents

Knowledge of the properties and working of these materials is of crucial importance to every painter. They have such a great influence on the painter's work that I shall discuss them in considerable detail.

Paints

Paint, as everyone knows, comes in tubes. It is not common knowledge, however, that some cheap, so-called student colors can actually be a great handicap because they are deficient in tinting strength. Several of the expensive pigments, the cadmiums, for example, as sold in cheaper brands, are considerably cut with inert material which gives the paint bulk at the expense of true color. Of course, all colors, even the most expensive ones, must contain a certain amount of an inert material, called "stabilizer," that allows the pigment and its vehicle—the oil— to remain in perfect suspension indefinitely while kept in tubes. The stabilizer gives the paint a certain "buttery" consistency, but at the same time it reduces its viscosity. This, in turn, deprives the paint of its capacity to blend properly. The lack of viscosity can be remedied by adding a conditioner, such as Copal Concentrate, described later.

Diluents

Paint sold in tubes is concentrated; that is, a minimum amount of the vehicle is used with the pigment in order to give the painter as much color substance as possible. However, usually, this thick color must be thinned by a painting medium prepared from linseed oil, stand oil, turpentine, and a hard resin known as copal. Such a painting medium, prepared according to my own formula, is called Copal Painting Medium. This medium is based on the formulas of the early Flemish masters, whose works have proven to be among the most stable of all the Old Masters and whose colors still possess undiminished brilliance. The advantage of using the copal media is demonstrated in the ease with which colors mixed with it can be blended and manipulated for impasti as well as for glazing and scumbling, see page 49.

Even so, the use of painting medium with tube colors is not the whole story. The body of the paint needs to be improved in regard to viscosity, depth of color, and capacity to fuse—that is, to blend sufficiently. Therefore, before starting to paint, one inch of every color to be used should first be thoroughly mixed with a small amount of Copal Concentrate—about as much as the tip of a painting knife will hold. This conditioner is also manufactured according to my own formula.

The heavy, honey-like substance should be scooped out of the bottle with the knife. White will require considerably more Concentrate than the rest of the colors, otherwise it will remain too stiff. Colors conditioned in this way will be flowing and glossy. (If too much Concentrate is added the colors will take on the consistency and characteristics common to enamel paint.) Arrange the conditioned colors on the palette in the order suggested on page 29. Then thin them with the painting medium to any desired degree.

Students may wonder why linseed oil and turpentine are not the appropriate media for thinning paint. The answer is simple. Linseed oil as such is the best vehicle used for binding the pigments that make our paint; turpentine, when used as a diluent, destroys the properties of this binder. But when turpentine is combined in the right proportions with a thermally processed linseed oil (stand oil) and a certain quality of natural resin, these ingredients, in combination, will yield the ideal paint diluent. Recipes calling for a mixture of damar varnish (soft resin) and linseed oil produce a compound that is deficient in point of permanence. Such recipes should be avoided.

Varnishes

I have referred to resin as an ingredient in mediums, conditioners, and varnishes. What are these resins? All resins are exudates of coniferous trees, but the resin referred to as "hard," called copal, is the product of trees that are now extinct. It is found in deposits in the earth. This hard resin is used as part of our painting medium. Damar is a soft resin suitable only in preparation of picture varnish. The word "varnish" denotes that a resin (hard or soft) has been dissolved in an appropriate volatile solvent, for example, turpentine or mineral spirits generally known as "painters' thinner."

Three kinds of varnishes are required in oil painting: Retouching Varnish, Damar Picture Varnish, and Copal Varnish. I recommend those manufactured according to my formulas.

Retouching Varnish is used for varnishing either freshly-finished paintings, or paintings less than six months old. Its first purpose is to bring out sunken colors that have dulled. Its second purpose is to protect the surface of the picture from dirt.

Damar Picture Varnish is prepared from a heavier concentration of resin. It is for paintings that have dried completely; this will usually be within six to 12 months after the painting has been finished, depending on the thickness of the paint film. Such a heavy final varnish will serve its purpose for many years, whereas a film of Retouching Varnish, because it is applied to paintings before they are thoroughly set, will disintegrate in a matter of months.

Copal Varnish is used on thoroughly dry paintings where a moderate gloss is desired. Its excellent lasting properties make it especially valuable for use on imprimatura, described in the chapter on alla prima painting. Because the composition of the commercial copal varnishes is not suitable for the purpose of varnishing and imprimatura, I always use Copal Varnish prepared according to my own formula.

Turpentine
We need turpentine, but for only two purposes. First, to soften semi-hardened paint (painters' thinner can also be used for this purpose), and second to prevent paint from "trickling," or "crawling" as it is sometimes called. There is no real explanation of why paint or the medium applied to an underlayer of paint occasionally contracts in little driblets like water on glass, instead of going on the surface evenly and

23

easily. Should this occur, however, turpentine brushed over the paint surface and then allowed to evaporate will promptly halt the trickling.

Drying Agents

Occasionally the artist may want paint to dry quickly so he can start overpainting with the least possible delay. Cobalt Dryer, **or** Cobalt Siccative, **is a liquid especially prepared to dry paint rapidly. Two drops added to one inch of color will make a thin application of paint dry in less than four hours. Drying will be equally accelerated if two drops of the dryer are added to a teaspoonful of the medium in the oil-cup—provided, of course, that all the colors are mixed with the medium.**

An important point to be remembered, however, is that dryers are not suitable for thick layers of paint. The dryer will not help thick paint dry quickly because it hardens the top film of paint first, which prevents air from reaching the paint underneath. For this reason, the dryer should be used only when painting thinly. Another point—excessive use of dryers is inadvisable; in time they will cause embrittlement and darkening of the paint film. Cobalt Siccative behaves better in this respect than other dryers.

Umber color, **because of its rapid-drying quality, will also act as a powerful drying agent when mixed with other colors, even in small quantities.**

Copal Painting Medium, Copal Concentrate, Retouching Varnish, Damar Picture Varnish and Copal Varnish, and Copal Siccative manufactured according to my formulas by Permanent Pigments, Cincinnati, Ohio, are available at good art supply stores everywhere.

Chapter 4.

The Colors

That the beauty of a painting depends to a large extent on the manner in which colors are used is self-evident. It follows that knowledge of colors and their general characteristics is of great importance, for without this knowledge the choice of colors becomes a guessing game—with wrong guesses usually in the majority.

To begin with, today the student can be sure that all standard colors are chemically compatible, and that adverse chemical reactions, not infrequent a half century or more ago, do not occur. Hence, when mixing colors our only concern is a sensible selection with which to achieve a required effect.

Suggested Palette
The beginner should start with a limited palette—a dozen or so colors in all. Of course, he may use only half as many, whether he is painting a portrait, a landscape, or a still life, but he should be familiar with a wider palette from which to make selections. The recommended colors can be seen on the color chart, Fig. 8, and a complete chart of color mixtures is shown in Figs. 9 and 10, pages 41 and 45.

The limited list of colors should include flake white, Prussian blue, ultramarine, and viridian green (the blues and greens are referred to as cold colors); and the warm range (the yellows, reds, and browns) represented by Naples yellow, light ochre, cadmium yellow light, cadmium red light, Venetian red, burnt siena, burnt umber, ivory black, and alizarin crimson.

General Characteristics of the Colors.
Flake white. **This is preferable to any other white because of its superior all-around properties. It dries well and is fairly opaque.**

The Blues. **Prussian blue has a greenish hue and possesses excellent** drying and tinting capacity. It is our most versatile, transparent color, useful on most occasions, except for portraiture. Ultramarine blue differs radically from Prussian blue in most respects except transparency. It is indispensable for portraiture and in landscape painting. In contrast to Prussian blue, ultramarine is purplish in hue.

The Greens. **Viridian green dries moderately well, is not too strong in tinting capacity, and is quite transparent. This color is indispensable in landscape and still life painting.**

The Yellows. **Naples yellow is a dense color of pale yellow hue. Of all the domestic manufacturers, only Permanent Pigments produces the genuine pigment sufficiently strong for most purposes.** Yellow ochre **(earth color) is fairly opaque, dries moderately well, and unlike Naples yellow, it has a warm tonality.** Cadmium yellow light **has a strong hue and good covering capacity, but it dries slowly. This color should always be of highest quality, for when adulterated it becomes weak and loses its value.**

The Reds. **Cadmium red light, the most brilliant red on our palette, should also be of highest quality.** Venetian red **is a pure red oxide of enormous tinting capacity and density. Colors possessing identical hue, but much weaker in tinting strength, are light red, terra rosa, and terra di Pozzuoli. These are earth colors and their mild hue makes them more suitable for use in portraiture than the strong Venetian red.**

The Browns. **Burnt siena is a rapid-drying reddish brown earth color of considerable strength. It has the valuable property of becoming very transparent when diluted with the medium.** Burnt umber, **the fastest drying color of all, is a dull, dense brown of considerable tinting strength.** Raw umber **is similar to burnt umber, but its tone is cooler, more grayish.**

Black Color. **Ivory black dries very slowly and although it is dense as a color, it does not have much body.**

Purple Color. **Alizarin crimson, the most transparent of all the colors, is** also the slowest drier. Its use is limited to special occasions, such as in painting flowers and draperies.

Several general characteristics emerge from the above descriptions: (1) tinting strength of colors, which, to a large degree, is responsible for covering capacity; (2) the drying properties which vary with colors—some colors requiring many days to dry, unless mixed with one of the fast driers, while other colors solidify in a matter of hours at normal room temperature; (3) the quality of opacity and transparency.

In order of tinting strength, Prussian blue and Venetian red come first, the cadmiums next. The rest of the colors are moderately strong. None of the colors on the list can be considered intrinsically weak in tinting capacity.

The best dryer is umber. Next comes burnt siena and Prussian blue. The poorest driers are black and alizarin crimson.

In the quality of transparency, alizarin crimson rates first place. Burnt siena, ultramarine blue, viridian green, and Prussian blue are all transparent, even when only lightly diluted with the medium. The most opaque colors are Venetian red, umber, and black (because of its dark hue). The transparent colors are referred to as glazing colors because they can be rendered transparent if they are sufficiently thinned with painting medium.

Part 2.

Painting Practice

Chapter 5.

Organizing the Palette,
Exercises with Brushes and Painting Knives

Organizing the Palette

Before starting our painting exercises, let us place our colors in logical order on the palette. Here is the traditional and most convenient order:

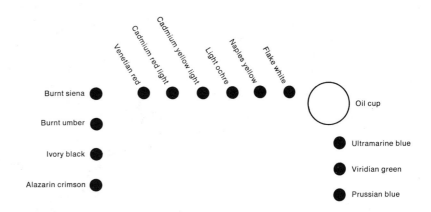

All the colors should be placed as closely to the edge of the palette as possible, to leave maximum free space for mixing.

Now with the palette ready for action—that is, with all the colors properly mixed with the Concentrate, as described on page 22, and placed on their assigned spaces, and with medium present in the oil cup—our first concern will be to familiarize ourselves with the working qualities of our tools.

Exercises with Brushes

Before attempting to paint a specific motif, students should exercise freely with all the brushes, both the sable group and the bristle group, in order to gain experience with their working qualities. Exercises can be done on a piece of cardboard or heavy paper treated with the commercial shellac thinned a little with denatured alcohol, to make it non-absorbent. The white synthetic glue in general use today, thinned considerably with water, can also be used for this purpose.

29

Figure 5.

A. Marks of round sable brushes

B. Marks of script liner and striper

Exercises involving random and varied brush strokes are excellent for getting the feel of the tools at our disposal. These exercises should be done in a completely relaxed mood with no attempt to represent any particular object.

First experiment with the sable brushes Numbers 1, 2, and 3. Always moisten brushes with the medium before dipping them into paint. This is our first procedure, and through this procedure the beginner will learn that the more the paint becomes diluted by the medium, the more easily it can be spread by the brush. In fact, the script liner and the striper will not function properly unless the paint is in a completely liquid condition. Only the largest of our sable brushes will operate satisfactorily with paint that is only slightly diluted. There is one exception, however— if paint is conditioned with Copal Concentrate until it is stringy, the small pointed sable brushes, especially the script liner and the striper, can be used to produce thin lines in high impasto as seen in Fig. 5.

If the entire group of sable brushes is tried for the exercises demonstrated in Fig. 5, it will be found that the Number 1 brush is useful only for short accurate strokes, straight or round, whereas the script liner, Number 5, is useful only for long, sweeping strokes. The Number 1 brush does not hold much paint and so must be dipped into paint frequently. The script liner, on the other hand, is capable of taking on infinitely more paint and therefore will be able to produce continuous, uninterrupted lines.

Figure 6.
Bristle brush marks

When experimenting with the bristle brushes, it will become apparent that those with short bristles will move even stiff paint that offers too much resistance to the long bristle brush. If bristles wear down through use, the brush should be discarded—short, worn-down bristles will not deposit paint on the canvas, but rather will scrape it off. I have often seen students trying desperately to apply paint to a canvas with an inadequate brush, totally unaware of the reason for their failure.

By painting a variety of strokes on our boards, Fig. 6, we will find out how differently bristle brushes and round sable brushes perform. Bristle brushes not only create a different paint texture in themselves, but they must also be handled differently; they cannot be effectively twisted and turned like round sable brushes. Their flat ferrule forces the hand to move the brush along its broad side. The narrow side of the bristle brush can be used for certain effects, but in practice this is seldom done.

Exercises with Painting Knives
In presenting the manipulation of painting knives, Fig. 7, descriptions and even illustrations seem inadequate. A few rules, however, can be established.

First we must know when the employment of a knife is indicated. It is indicated whenever canvas is used as a support. Painting knives are not suitable for work on panels. Panels are rigid and this makes the use of a knife awkward because there is no rapport between the vibrating blade and the rigid surface. Neither does the knife work well on toothless surfaces, that is, surfaces that are perfectly smooth; here the knife is inclined to slide and slither. This happens because the knife, in manipulating the paint, cannot force some of the paint into the interstices of the fabric.

Figure 7.
Painting knife marks

Then, the viscosity of the paint must be taken into account. Viscous paint has a heavier body and this makes it particularly suitable for handling with the knife, as explained on page 22.

In addition to the character of the support and the viscosity of the paint the nature of the knife blade must be considered. It cannot be overemphasized that the blade must have just the right degree of elasticity. A stiff blade requires extra pressure which makes the mass of paint squeeze out from under it. An overelastic blade, on the other hand, does not have the power to move the paint efficiently. Short narrow blades, useful for certain manipulations, are not as well adapted for blending and smoothing out large surfaces as the wider and longer blades, see **Fig. 3.**

To become familiar with the working of the knives, students should practice on pieces of waste canvas placed on a soft support such as a pile of newspaper. Stretchers are unnecessary. In order to emphasize what I said before about canvas and knife work, I will repeat that only canvas should be used when working with knives. The smooth surface of cardboard, such as we employed for exercises with the brushes, will not provide the proper conditions for exercises with painting knives.

The knives I recommend for beginners were described in Chapter 1 and pictured in Fig. 3, page 14. Knives that are radically different in construction are not advisable for the exercises suggested here.

The three knives shown should be used in succession, alternately applying more and less pressure to the canvas. Soon it will be clear that when the knife is held at a certain angle, it leaves considerable paint on the surface, and that a different angle is better for spreading the paint thinly. However, it is not only a particular angle of the knife that is responsible for the effect achieved, but also, in a large measure, it is the amount of pressure applied. Pushing a thin layer of paint into the interstices of grainy fabric requires greater pressure than moving paint on fabric with comparatively little grain.

When scraping a thin layer of surplus paint from the surface of a canvas, hold the edge of the knife at a narrow angle, fairly close to the canvas. Exert appreciable pressure and always move the knife away from yourself, rather than toward yourself. For blending large surfaces, and to produce smooth surfaces, the blade of the knife should rest flat or almost flat on the canvas. Knife Number 2 should be used for this purpose. When blending colors, it is imperative to wipe the blade after every stroke and clean off all clinging paint.

To produce strong color effects by means of a knife, two or more colors should be taken up on the blade and, with little or no previous mixing, applied to the canvas in a few strokes. The longer the colors are worked with the knife the more thoroughly they become intermixed—and hence the duller they will look.

While practicing these exercises, the beginner may observe that he is able to produce extraordinary coloristic and textural effects similar to effects seen in the works of skillful painters. This could suggest that such effects may result from the particular nature of the instrument and the intrinsic beauty of the colors, rather than from the virtuosity of the artist. In saying this, however, I do not mean to imply that mastery in the use of painting knives can be achieved effortlessly. As a matter of fact, I would like to caution students against thinking that isolated effects, often largely accidental, indicate adequate proficiency. At this point in our progress, much still remains to be learned.

Chapter 6.	Mixing Colors

A complete showing of colors is reproduced in Fig. 8, Chart 1, accompanied by a descriptive listing. A showing of 56 color intermixtures is reproduced in Figs. 9 and 10, Charts 2 and 3, accompanied by a descriptive listing.

The mixing exercises were prepared in this way:

On each square, first two colors, see Chart 2, were thoroughly intermixed. Next, the same colors were only slightly intermixed. Then white was added to the mixture. Thus on squares 1 to 56 all the colors on Chart 1 were intermixed—using only two colors at a time, with white on the right edge. All applications were made with a painting knife because the individual colors used in the mixtures would be less distinguishable if mixed with a brush.

There can be no doubt that without an initial familiarity with the characteristics of colors the student would have to rely on guess work. Fumbling would be the inevitable result. Therefore I think it is advisable at this point to repeat a few important facts covering both the limited and the extended palette.

Limited Palette

Blue. **The only blue suitable for painting flesh is ultramarine. Of course this blue can also be used in landscape painting for greens, skies, and other areas. But in mixtures with warm colors it will produce purplish tones. Prussian blue on the other hand yields greenish tonalities and possesses an altogether much more aggressive hue.**

Green. **Viridian, the only unmixed green, can be looked upon as a blue-green, inasmuch as it does not belong to the yellow-green family. It is universally useful in landscape and still life painting.**

Yellow. **The only yellow suitable for flesh tints is yellow ochre; it is also the warmest and mildest yellow on our palette. Naples yellow, also a low-keyed color, is suitable only for atmospheric effects, that is, distant planes and skies. Cadmium yellow (light, medium, or dark) is very strong; hence it will serve well for greens in landscapes and still lifes.**

Red. **Venetian red, or light red, because of its low key is the only red suitable for flesh tints. The brilliant cadmium red is useful in painting flowers, draperies, and the like. Burnt siena is a brownish red used chiefly in landscapes.**

Brown. **Umber, raw or burnt. Burnt umber is a warm brownish-red, raw umber is cooler in tone. Umber is our only brown color. It is used for flesh tints, and in general to darken any other color or color combination. As we know, it yields a black in mixtures with ultramarine or Prussian blue.**

Black. **Ivory black is just plain black,excellent for greens in mixtures with yellow.**

Purple. **Alizarin crimson. Its use is quite limited; it is employed chiefly for painting flowers.**

Extended Palette
Blue. **Phthalo blue is a clear neutral blue not as useful as Prussian blue but interesting to experiment with. Cerulean blue is greenish, rather opaque. Appropriate for skies.**

Green. **Phthalo green is not unlike viridian but more brilliant and "acidy" in color. Because of its aggressive hue it is of limited value. Chromoxide green opaque is a dense, dull color, occasionally suitable for portrait backgrounds and in landscapes.**

Yellow. **Mars yellow and raw siena resemble ochre superficially. Mars yellow is more transparent; raw siena is darker in tint. Both are suitable** in landscape painting. Zinc yellow has greenish tonality, valuable for still lifes.

Black. **Mars black is much more dense than ivory black, dries quickly and is not as generally adaptable. But where powerful accents are required, it can be very useful.**

Purple. **Mars violet is a dark red-violet, extremely opaque, and very interesting to experiment with.**

The principle of color mixing is this: always endeavor to obtain a wanted color effect by employing as few colors as possible. In addition to white, two or at the most three colors should be enough to produce any desirable nuance. A combination of four colors (and white) is unusual. Furthermore, if the painter mixes many colors together, he could have difficulty remembering how he produced a certain satisfying effect and will find it hard to duplicate this effect at will.

Intermixtures of Neutral Colors
As I pointed out earlier, the more thoroughly one compounds the colors the more thoroughly the pigment particles become interspersed, hence the duller the total effect will appear to the eye. **On the other hand, brief mixing of different colors will preserve their brilliance.**

White added to one or a combination of colors will always reduce the intensity of the hues, and the more white is added the more pastel-like the color becomes, eventually becoming chalky in appearance.

Figure 8. Chart 1 — The Colors, see facing page

1.	2.	3.	4.	5.
Naples yellow	ochre	Mars yellow	raw siena	zinc yellow

6.	7.	8.	9.	10.
cadmium yellow light	cadmium yellow dark	cadmium yellow orange	cadmium red light	Venetian red

11.	12.	13.	14.	15.
Mars violet	alizarin crimson	siena burnt	umber burnt	Prussian blue

16.	17.	18.	19.	20.
phthalo blue	ultramarine blue	cerulean blue	phthalo green	viridian green

21.	22.	23.	24.
chrome oxide green	white	ivory black	Mars black

However, in point of quantity used, white outranks by far all the other colors; hence the standard tube of white bought in art stores is much larger than any of the other tubes of colors. In weight, it may be four to eight times as heavy as an equal quantity of some of the other colors.

White is essential in producing neutral tones which, more often than not, make up the major areas of most paintings conceived in the classical style. (As we learned earlier, a neutral tone is one deprived of its high hue.)

Neutral tones can be predominantly gray, green, pink, or brown, see Fig. 10, Chart 3. Under "gray" so many variants can be conceived that it seems practically impossible to enumerate them all. I suggest that students, using a piece of white cardboard as described on page 29, produce a variety of grays by mixing colors in the following order:

Grays. **Prussian blue, umber, and white. Depending on the quantitative relations of these colors, silvery bluish or brownish grays, light or dark in tone, can be obtained. Combinations of these two colors are more varied and have a wider range than any other mixtures that may yield a gray color.**

Different grays can be obtained from:
   Viridian green, umber, and white.
   Ultramarine, umber, and white.
   Green, red, and white.

The last combination differs from the first in that "green" can be a mixture of a great variety of colors. Regarding red, we have three kinds on our palette: Venetian red, cadmium red, burnt siena. Any one of these can be used, depending on the occasion. It should be rememberd that green and red are complimentary colors and as such, theoretically, they cancel one another, which means that they lose their identity. Greens will be discussed in detail below.

42   Now, however, before we go on to the greens, let me explain why I have

not mentioned the most obvious gray, namely, the one resulting from a mixture of black and white. The reason for this is that such a gray has little value for us. Furthermore, when using Prussian blue, or ultramarine and umber, we actually operate with black for either of these color combinations appears perfectly black until white is added. And in adding white to these mixtures, both nuances—the brown as well as blue —emerge subtly, thus yielding color values such as black and white could never produce.

44

Figure 9. Chart 2 — Color Mixtures , see facing page

1.
Naples
yellow

cadmium
red light

2.
Naples
yellow

Mars
violet

3.
Naples
yellow

alizarin
crimson

4.
Naples
yellow

burnt
siena

5.
Naples
yellow

burnt
umber

6.
Naples
yellow

ivory
black

7.
Naples
yellow

Prussian
blue

8.
Naples
yellow

viridian
green

9.
Naples
yellow

chrome
oxide green

10.
ochre

cadmium
red light

11.
ochre

Venetian
red

12.
ochre

burnt
siena

13.
ochre

burnt
umber

14.
ochre

black

15.
ochre

Prussian
blue

16.
ochre

ultramarine
blue

17.
ochre

viridian
green

18.
zinc
yellow

cadmium
red light

19.
zinc
yellow

alizarin
crimson

20.
zinc
yellow

burnt
siena

21.
zinc
yellow

black

22.
zinc
yellow

viridian
green

23.
cadmium
yellow

cadmium
red

24.
cadmium
yellow

Mars
violet

25.
cadmium
yellow

alizarin
crimson

26.
cadmium
yellow

burnt
siena

27.
cadmium
yellow

burnt
umber

28.
cadmium
yellow

black

29.
cadmium
yellow

Prussian
blue

30.
cadmium
yellow

ultramarine
blue

31.
cadmium
yellow

viridian
green

32.
cadmium
yellow

chrome
oxide green

33.
cadmium
red

Mars
violet

34.
cadmium
red

alizarin
crimson

35.
cadmium
red

burnt
umber

36.
cadmium
red

black

37.
cadmium
red

Prussian
blue

38.
cadmium
red

ultramarine
blue

39.
Venetian
red

burnt
umber

40.
Venetian
red

black

41.
Venetian
red

Prussian
blue

42.
Venetian
red

ultramarine
blue

43.
Venetian
red

viridian
green

44.
Venetian
red

chrome
oxide green

45.
Mars
violet

black

46.
Mars
violet

chrome
oxide green

47.
alizarin
crimson

ultramarine
blue

48.
alizarin
crimson

viridian
green

49.
burnt
siena

ultramarine
blue

50.
burnt
siena

Prussian
blue

51.
burnt
siena

viridian
green

52.
burnt
umber

Prussian
blue

53.
burnt
umber

ultramarine
blue

54.
Prussian
blue

viridian
green

55.
Prussian
blue

chrome
oxide green

56.
viridian
green

cerulean
blue

Figure 10. Chart 3 — Neutral Tones , see facing page

1.
gray

2.
green

3.
pink

Greens. **The greens discussed here are prepared with large quantities of white to render them neutral, because if only a little white were used, the hue of the mixture would appear too strong to be called "neutral." I have referred to the endless variety of grays. Almost the same could be stated in regard to green. Green is always a result of mixing a yellow color with brown, blue, or black. This, of course, leads to an enormous range of greens. Now let's try to enumerate some of them:**

Bluish greens—

Prussian blue, umber, cadmium yellow, and white.

Prussian blue, umber, ochre and white.

Prussian blue, umber, Naples yellow, and white.

Additional variations: bluish green can be obtained by using ultramarine or viridian green instead of Prussian blue.

Grayish greens—

Black, ochre, and white.

Black, cadmium yellow and white.

Black, Naples yellow and white.

Brownish greens—

Umber, cadmium yellow and white.

Pink Tones. **A pink color results from a mixture of a red, such as cadmium red, Venetian red, or burnt siena (which is really a brown-red), with either white or Naples yellow, or both.**

When I refer to cadmium red, I mean specifically the light variety, for the darker cadmium reds mixed with white will yield purplish nuances very much like those produced by alizarin crimson. The brightest "floral" pink can be obtained from cadmium red and white; with the addition of Naples yellow the tone will be still more delicate. Pinks produced from Venetian red and white will be duller, hence more neutral, and those from burnt siena and white will be the dullest of all.

Brown Tones. **A mixture of white and umber will yield the dullest neutral grayish brown. Livelier brown tones can be achieved by adding either burnt siena or ochre, or both, to the mixture.**

Let me make a useful observation here. My reference to "dull" or "neutral" colors should not be taken as a negative qualification, for at times neutral colors play just as important a role in the make up of a painting as the brilliant ones.

Intermixtures of Brilliant Colors

Because white, as stated before, cuts the intensity of a color's hue, its use should be avoided when great brilliance of color is desirable. "Intensity" and "brilliance" are not synonymous, for a brilliant color must of necessity be light, whereas an intense blue, for example, can be of a darker nuance.

Yellow-orange-red. **Cadmium yellow is the most brilliant yellow color. Any admixture of another yellow such as ochre or Naples yellow will lower its hue. When mixing cadmium red with cadmium yellow, an orange will result.**

Cadmium red, light. **This is the most brilliant red, and only an admixture of alizarin crimson will allow it to retain its brilliance, although this admixture will inject a purplish hue. The result of such a mixture is identical with cadmium red medium, or the color designated as cadmium red dark, depending on the amount of alizarin crimson present in the mixture.**

Purple Colors. **These are mixtures of red and blue, specifically cadmium red and/or alizarin crimson and ultramarine. Mauve or violet colors are simply purple mixtures combined with white.**

Green Colors. **The most brilliant green is obtained from a mixture of viridian green and cadmium yellow. Next in brilliance is a mixture of cadmium yellow and ultramarine, or cadmium yellow and Prussian blue, or cadmium yellow and black. Cadmium yellow and umber will also produce a lively green in a lower key.**

Blue Colors. **Both Prussian blue and ultramarine are transparent; therefore** they cannot be used without an admixture of an opaque color for representation of sky, water, distant mountains, flowers, or what have you. However, the admixture of white will not dull these colors. On the contrary, it will intensify their hues. In fact, Prussian blue and white will appear so fiercely blue that it can hardly be used without dulling it with umber or some other color, as the occasion may require. Ultramarine and white will also produce an intense opaque blue, on the purplish side.

Chapter 7.

Glazing and Scumbling

Glazing

Fig. 11. Chart 4. Impasto is the application of colors with appreciable thickness. This makes the colors opaque and therefore the underlying color will not show through the impasto. All our exercises thus far were done with more or less opaque colors applied with greater or lesser impasto (thickness).

If the underlying color asserts itself through the layer of color on top of it, the top color of course must be transparent. Referring to transparent colors, we stated that blues, viridian green, and especially alizarin crimson are transparent. When thinly applied, even without prior dilution by the medium, these colors will be semi-transparent, although in the case of Prussian blue the dark hue tends to obscure the surface on which it rests. However, with the exception of white, every one of our colors can be made transparent to any desired degree if sufficiently diluted. For example, burnt siena, the most glowing color, is opaque and dull in its natural state, but when it is sufficiently thinned by the medium it becomes quite transparent. It is important to remember that true glazes never contain white because even a trace of white color will destroy the value and transparency of a dark glaze. Of course the underlying color must always be dry before glazing.

Since transparence allows the underlying color to show through in varying degrees, it follows that the character of this underlying color will, to some extent, influence the overlying color. As a matter of fact, this influence can be so great in some instances that the superimposed color loses its identity. For example, when using black, thinned by the medium, over yellow, the black will not look black—the total effect will be green. The same principle applies to viridian green or the blues when they are used as a glaze over yellow—they will all be conditioned by the underlying yellow color to a point where their original hue becomes unrecognizable.

49

On previous occasions I referred to the brilliance of certain colors. However, brilliance such as can be produced by means of glazing is unattainable when using a color opaquely. The examples of glazing shown in Fig. 11 clearly demonstrate this fact. Only a few examples are reproduced but they are characteristic of the possibilities to which the manipulation of glazes lends itself.

Scumbling

Fig. 12. Chart 5. We have defined a glaze as an application of a darker, transparent color to a light (dry) underpainting. A "scumble" is just the opposite. This manipulation calls for the application of a lighter color on top of a darker color in such a fashion as to keep the dark underlying color evident. Thus the light color must be transparent to a certain degree in order to allow the dark color to assert itself.

Moreover, whereas glazes can be executed only on a dry surface, scumbling can be applied (1) into a wet glaze, (2) into a wet thin opaque color, (3) into a wet impasto color, and (4) onto a dry (but oiled) underpainting. In the first three instances I said "into" in the fourth "onto," simply because when painting a wet color on top of another wet color, the colors will combine in a lesser or greater degree. This is not so when painting onto a dry surface; here the two coats of paint do not mingle; they remain completely independent. In cases numbers 1, 2, and 3 a scumble cannot be carried out very well with a brush, for the brush would simply brush away the underlying wet coat. Hence, only a painting knife is effective for this manipulation. However, on a dry (but oiled) underpainting a brush works better than a knife.

Which colors are suitable for scumbling? Any light color can be used provided that it rests on a darker color. In contrast to the glazes—for which proper conditions must be created in advance—scumbling can be done at any time as it does not require a dry surface. In the course of every painting scumbling enters into play for whenever the painter mixes a thin light color into a darker color he "scumbles." In the still life painting (Fig. 17), these characteristic effects are seen on the basket where a light scumble of ochre and white was painted into a wet glaze of umber. Other scumbles are seen in the background where the light color was painted into a solid wet layer of paint. In both instances a painting knife was used.

Since we are now approaching the actual task of painting, it should be stated that one does not paint—ever—on a truly "dry" surface, for, before painting, the surface upon which one works must always first be "oiled" by the medium. This is done to facilitate the movement of the brush, to make the colors spread more easily, and to promote a better adhesion of paint.

"Oiling" means brushing the medium sparingly onto the dry surface to be overpainted. Large surfaces can be oiled most efficiently by means of a lint free material such as cheesecloth. However, between underpaintings there is no need to oil surfaces because in this case it would serve no useful purpose.

Figure 11. Chart 4 — Glazing , see facing page

1.

Underpainting:
gray

glaze:
burnt siena

2.

Underpainting:
gray

glaze:
viridian green

3.

Underpainting:
gray

glaze:
alizarin crimson

4.

Underpainting:
gray

glaze:
burnt umber

5.

Underpainting:
yellow

glaze:
alizarin crimson

6.

Underpainting:
yellow

glaze:
burnt siena

7.

Underpainting:
yellow

glaze:
viridian green

8.

Underpainting:
yellow

glaze:
black

9.

Underpainting:
pink

glaze:
burnt siena

10.

Underpainting:
pink

glaze:
viridian green

11.

Underpainting:
red

glaze:
viridian green

12.

Underpainting:
red

glaze:
alizarin crimson

13.

Underpainting:
red

glaze:
burnt siena

14.

Underpainting:
red

glaze:
black

15.

Underpainting:
blue

glaze:
burnt siena

16.

Underpainting:
blue

glaze:
alizarin crimson

Figure 12. Chart 5 — Scumbling , see facing page

Black background

1.

ultramarine blue
and white

2.

cadmium red

3.

umber
and white

4.

burnt siena
and white

5.

cadmium yellow

6.

ochre
and white

Red background

1.

ultramarine blue
and white

2.

viridian green
and white

3.

alizarin crimson
and white

4.

burnt siena
and white

5.

cadmium yellow

6.

ochre

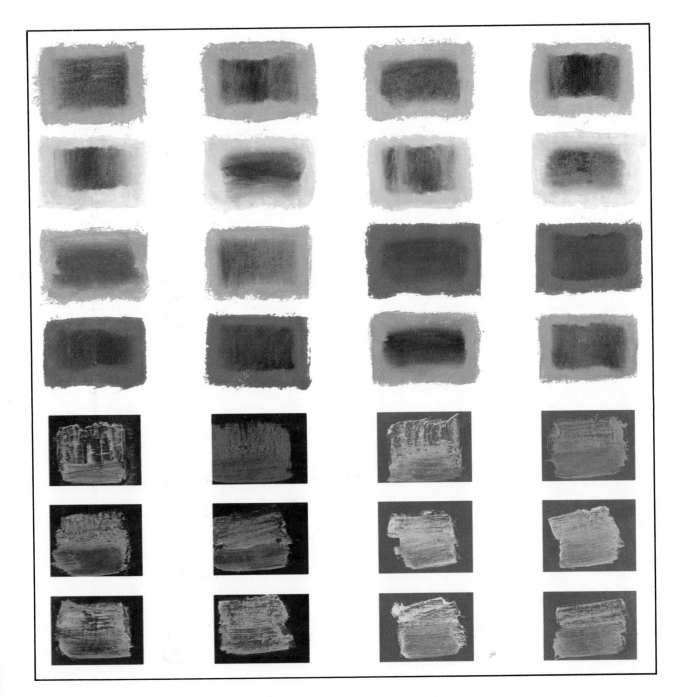

Part 3.

Painting a Picture

Chapter 8.

The Alla Prima Technique

Now at last we shall be facing our first attempt at representation. But before undertaking this, the following question should be decided: Shall we use the alla prima method, or shall we paint on an underpainting? These two methods are at our disposal. We shall discuss them in detail.

Alla Prima Painting
This term means completing a painting in one operation, wet-into-wet, and aiming to achieve the final coloristic effects at once. **To explain further:** When the object to be painted appears red, we employ the red at once, whereas when we "underpaint" the red object may be given an initial coat of gray, or green, or some other color. Moreover, alla prima painting, because it is done wet-in-wet, must be finished while it is still wet. Therefore the total working period spent on such a painting will seldom be more than a day. As a rule, small panels are used for this technique; suitable sizes range from about 7 by 10 to 16 by 20 inches. A panel within such modest proportions can be finished in a very short time. In fact, in all my experience, every beginner using the alla prima method was able to cover his panel during one short morning session (not always, of course, to the best advantage). Generally speaking, alla prima work is done in a sketchy manner, but if the artist wishes he can go into minute details.

Although I stated that an alla prima painting "must" be finished in one operation while it is still wet, this not not an inflexible rule. Minor corrections and modifications can be executed after the painting is finished and dry, but this should not be done habitually, for, as the practice will show, it is not a "happy" measure.
The step-by-step procedure for alla prima painting is as follows:

The Imprimatura
For a support, a Masonite panel is our best choice. The panel, carrying the gesso ground as described on page 19, should be given an

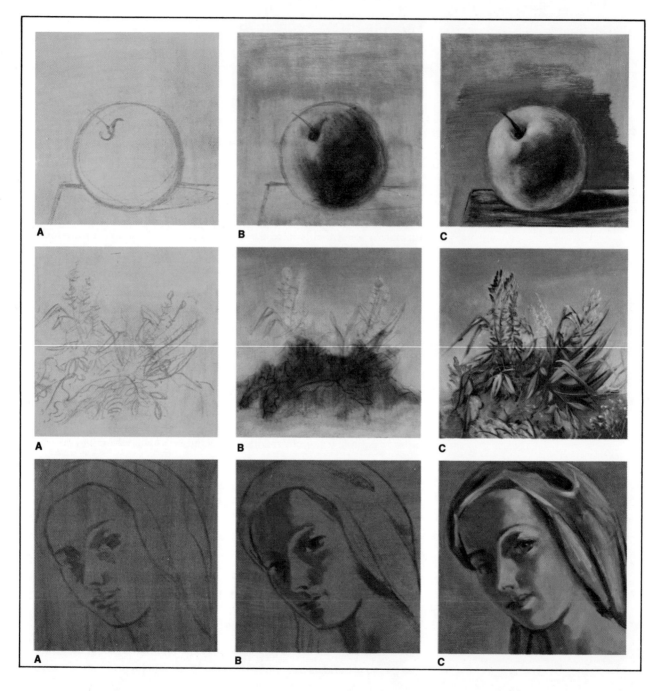

A

B

C

A

B

C

A

B

C

application of a transparent color—the so-called imprimatura—prepared from any one of these: burnt siena, viridian green, cadmium yellow, ochre, or umber, thinned to watercolor consistency by Copal Varnish.

The five principal colors useful for imprimatura listed above are not arbitrary choices; the choice is governed by the subject matter one intends to paint. More about this later. Now this initial color, the imprimatura, must be dry before work is done on top of it—as a matter of fact, the imprimatura will be dry to the touch in a matter of minutes, but complete solidification takes at least two days. When siccative is used, see page 24, two drops to one teaspoonful of varnish will solidify the imprimatura in one day. Because of the drying time involved, it is a good idea to have at hand a supply of imprimatura-covered panels in different colors, prepared in advance. Then you will be ready to paint a picture whenever you wish, without being delayed by waiting for the imprimatura to dry.

Damar varnish is not suitable for imprimatura, for it never solidifies sufficiently to resist the solving action of the Copal Painting Medium (which, as we remember, contains turpentine) used over it. Linseed oil is totally inappropriate for this purpose.

Before starting to paint, a drawing of the subject matter should be done on either the surface of the white gesso or on the imprimatura. Vine charcoal is best for this. After the drawing is finished, fixative should be used to render it indelible, see page 20.

Next, the panel should be moistened with Copal Painting Medium Heavy (this is especially suitable for alla prima work). Do this just before painting, using a bristle brush. All the colors should be conditioned with Copal Concentrate. This is particularly important in alla prima work for here glazes prevail and the concentrate adds body and strength to thin paint used for that purpose.

Now we are ready to begin our work. First let us consider the colors

Figure 13.
A Still Life in Alla Prima.
A simple demonstration of glazing and scumbling

Figure 14.
Field Flowers in Alla Prima

Figure 15.
A Head Study in Alla Prima

57

Enlargement of Figure 13 C

Enlargement of Figure 14 C

of our panels and chose the one most suitable for the task at hand. When painting fruit or flowers, for example, the final colors will be kept in a high key. Here experience will teach us the following: the key of the final color will be higher when the color of the imprimatura is brighter. And, since yellow is the brightest color, let us start painting such subject matter on a yellow imprimatura.

A Still Life Step-By-Step
The apple shown in Figs. 13 A, B, C was painted in one operation on a cadmium yellow imprimatura in the following manner:

Step 1, Fig. 13A. The entire surface of the panel was glazed with viridian green, the red area of the apple was thinly covered by alizarin crimson.

Step 2, Fig. 13B. Next, the shadow of the apple was darkened by applying ultramarine blue and alizarin crimson to the area.

Step 3, Fig. 13C. The highlight was produced by simply wiping off the alizarin crimson color with cheesecloth so as to reveal the underlying yellow color. For the background, umber, viridian green, and white were used. The table was painted with an umber color, strengthened by ultramarine in the shadow area.

In all, six colors were used in this sketch, and the following brushes were employed: the large round sable brush, the script liner, and two of the smaller bristle brushes. The size of the panel is 9 by 9 inches.

Field Flowers Step-By-Step
Figs. 14, A, B, C show a more complicated motif—a clump of field flowers. The panel is 9 by 9 inches. Here is the painting procedure:

Step 1, Fig. 14A. A charcoal drawing was done on a cadmium yellow imprimatura. Fixative was sprayed on the drawing to make it indelible.

59

Step 2, Fig. 14B. After oiling the panel with the medium, the sky was painted with Prussian blue, umber, and white, with Naples yellow used in the lower areas. A glaze of burnt siena and Prussian blue was spread on the area where the plants are densely grouped. Then, using a script liner, the details were reestablished with burnt siena and Prussian blue strongly diluted by the medium.

Step 3, Fig. 14C. This is the finished painting. It was executed spontaneously, and, as becomes evident when comparing A with B, the details were improvised rather than methodically elaborated. This manner of painting imparts freshness and speeds progress— in fact, it did not take more than 20 minutes to do the painting from start to finish. Of course the properly prepared background made such rapid work possible. The entire procedure demonstrates that painting wet-in-wet is the method best suited for spontaneous rendition. Were we to allow stage B to dry in, this would have made it impossible to finish the panel in alla prima technique.

Eight colors, all conditioned by Copal Concentrate, were used: white, Prussian blue, viridian green, Naples yellow, cadmium yellow, cadmium red, burnt siena, and alizarin crimson.

Bristle brushes were used for the initial painting in B, and a script liner was used for the delineations. The final painting was done with medium and large round sable brushes, and the script liner.

Much of the original imprimatura remains in evidence in the finished painting, as can be seen. The hair-fine impasto lines were done with paint containing large additions of Copal Concentrate.

A Head Study Step-By-Step
Figs. 15 A, B, C. The panel is 9 by 9 inches. The imprimatura is burnt siena.

Step 1, Fig. 15A. The charcoal drawing, rendered indelible with fixative.

Step 2, Fig. 15B. The shadows, mixed from white, umber, Venetian red, and a little ultramarine, were painted after oiling the panel with the medium. The drawing was strengthened, using a small round sable brush and umber strongly diluted with the medium. The color of the shadows appears rather cool here because it contrasts with the glowing red imprimatura of the panel.

Step 3, Fig. 15C. The colors on the light part of the face were obtained by mixing ochre, white, and a little umber. After this part was painted, light and shade were blended together. At this stage the final touches were applied—shadows were strengthened, highlights added, and details of the features elaborated. The viscosity of the paint conditioned by the Concentrate and thinned by the Copal Painting Medium made the blending safe and effortless, even when using a harsh bristle brush.

Next, the headdress was painted. First a glaze of viridian green was spread over the entire surface. Into this glaze went dark accents of umber and Prussian blue. The light pink color of the headdress is a mixture of white and Venetian red. The final colors of the background are umber, Prussian blue, and white. As soon as these "cold" colors were spread over the burnt siena imprimatura, the tonality of the head looked much warmer.

The following brushes were used: The painting was started with the Number 7 bristle brush and a small round sable brush for the drawing. Then a second bristle brush of the same size was used for painting the light areas. Next, the first brush, wiped clean, served for blending. The large round sable brush was chosen for details of the features— the eyes, nostrils, and mouth. The headdress and the background were painted with the bristle brush, and the final touches on the head and the headdress were made with the script liner.

Mountain Landscape Step-By-Step

Fig. 16 shows an alla prima landscape executed on a panel 12 by 16 inches, carrying on ochre imprimatura.

Step 1. A charcoal drawing was done on the imprimatura and rendered indelible with fixative.

Step 2. In accordance with classical landscape painting procedure, the most distant plane was the first to be dealt with—in this instance, the sky. Here viridian green was mixed with a little ultramarine and white in the upper areas. Naples yellow was used in the lower area with traces of viridian green appearing here and there. The middle ground, the mountain section, was painted with Prussian blue, ochre, and some umber; the rest of the ground was done with ochre, viridian green, cadmium yellow, and Prussian blue. For the foliage, burnt siena and Prussian blue were used for the dark sections; cadmium yellow and white for the light effects. Only six colors, and white, were employed.

In this painting, it is obvious that the script liner and the striper played a dominant role. These brushes and a larger round sable brush were responsible for creating the scaffolding of the composition.

When we examine all our examples done in alla prima technique, one characteristic stands out—glazes predominate and the imprimatura remains in evidence in many spots throughout the entire picture, unifying the tonality of the whole. **Moreover, the treatment is sketchy, and this lends an impression of freshness and spontaneity.**

Comments on the Colors used in our Alla Prima Work
First let us consider still life painting, particularly fruits and flowers. Here, our entire palette with the exception of the so-called "non-flowery" colors—that is, umber, black, and ochre—can be used. In painting backgrounds there is no such restriction as neutral backgrounds will always compliment colorful elements of the main motifs. However, depending on one's particular conception, it is feasible to have the entire surface—background and all—carry strong colors.

Our next example was the head study. Here four colors in addition to white were used. Never deviate from this color scheme when a more or less realistic portrait presentation seems desirable **because all these colors are compatible and can be combined and recombined in any manner without danger of becoming muddy.**

Therefore, for emphasis, I will repeat that this choice of colors can be considered foolproof: umber, light red (the earth color, not cadmium red!), ochre, and ultramarine, in addition to white, for painting shadows; white and ochre for the light tones. Should the light areas appear too glaring, a touch of umber will lower their key.

With these four colors any desirable tonality can be established by mixing less of this, or more of the other. For example, when more of the ochre and light red is used and less ultramarine, or no ultramarine at all, a warm color scheme will result. On the other hand, when the red color is omitted or used very sparingly, a cool tone will prevail. Umber always darkens colors; ochre livens them up. Ultramarine cools the colors. In the presence of umber, ultramarine will gray the colors down; and in the presence of red it will make the tones appear purplish; when some ochre is added this nuance, in turn, will quickly disappear. Umber mixed with ultramarine will yield a deep black. It is clear then, from the above, that complexions of any conceivable color can be produced with this scheme. (When painting black or dark brown complexions as those of Negroes, however, burnt siena should be used instead of the
light red.)

Figure 16.
Mountain Landscape in
Alla Prima

Another matter that needs to be discussed is painting hair. Our four chosen colors will require only one additional color to cover all possible hair tones. This additional color is burnt siena and it will be used for painting red hair.

Now, to produce the various colors of hair, our selection of five colors should be used in the following way: for blond hair, ochre and white for light tones, with an addition of umber for deeper shades; umber and burnt siena for brown hair; burnt siena and ochre for red hair; umber and ultramarine for black hair—and when white is added to this mixture we get a gray color for gray hair.

Students may ask "and how about the color of the lips?" Here is my advice. Beware of using cadmium red or alizarin crimson—the colors of flamboyant lipsticks. These give the lips a hard poster-like appearance. Venetian red for the middle tone with an addition of white for the light tones and an addition of umber for the darkest parts in shade will serve the purpose well.

And finally, for the eyes any desired color can be obtained from a combination of the same colors used in painting flesh. However, it should always be kept in mind that the light areas—whether it is the high-light in the pupil or, especially, the white of the eye—should be painted in a lower key than that seen on the model, for nothing is more distressing in a portrait than enamel-like eye whites or the piercing look produced by a glaring pupil.

Our last example in alla prima painting, the mountain landscape, posed a different problem, that of treating objects placed in the foreground, middle ground, and distance. This involves two aspects of perspective: the linear and the atmospheric.

Linear perspective refers to the phenomenon that the further objects recede into the background, the smaller they will look to us. Much fuss has been made about this so-called empirical or scientific perspective, and many a volume was written about this system after its invention early in the 15th century. The system soon grew to be of paramount importance in painting. But the original rigid precepts became greatly modified during the period of the Baroque and eventually lost much of the significance and meaning they once possessed.

The second aspect of perspective, "atmospheric" perspective, is simple and is still valid today. The principles involved rely on the fact that colors change their appearance as they move beyond our proximate vision, and this change becomes more pronounced with the increase of distance. Hence even the strongest red or yellow local colors will fade out on the horizon to a pale greenish or bluish hue. In other words, distance drains the color progressively of its intensity. This principle is exemplified in Fig. 16. However, in styles where a realistic representation is not the artist's concern, the principles of atmospheric perspective are not necessarily taken into account.

Although above I referred to "principles," the student, once he becomes aware of the nature of these principles, need not follow them blindly. In certain instances, because of some vagaries or contingencies of composition, an adjustment of the principles may be justified.

As I have pointed out before, alla prima technique—the easiest to master —is essentially a sketchy procedure. A more elaborate method is discussed in the next chapter, "The Underpainting Technique."

Figure 17.
A Still Life Painting on an
Underpainting

A. Underpainting

B. Finished Painting

Chapter 9.

The Underpainting Technique

What is an "underpainting"? Any layer of paint under the final layer could be considered an underpainting; as such, it could be an unfinished painting, or a finished but unsuccessful painting that needs to be overpainted. But when we talk about "the underpainting method," we mean a purposefully established underpainting that contributes toward the final effect of the finished painting.

General Principles of Underpainting

(1) Canvas rather than a panel should be used because of the mechanics involved in this painting technique. Paint should be applied with a painting knife in order to push it into the interstices of the fabric. If small areas are to be painted that cannot be successfully done with a painting knife, a brush should be used first but after the brush has done its work the knife should be used to tone down the heavy texture of the brush strokes and to fill the interstices of the canvas. Otherwise the texture of the brush strokes in the underpainting may interfere with superimposed brush strokes, creating unpleasant textural effects.

(2) The paint used should be rather stiff, that is, dilution by the medium should be avoided in order to create a solid substratum that will add support and substance to the superimposed paint. If a heavier texture appears to be desirable, a second, third, or more underpaintings may follow, but each underpainting layer must be applied on a perfectly dry surface. Paint used for this purpose should have "body," that is, the paint should not be transparent; this condition is, of course, theoretical because in practice all the colors used will be intermixed with white to a large degree, and white has more solidity and body than any other paint. (As we learned earlier, the pigment-oil relation in flake white is 10:1; in other paints it will be up to 1:1.)

(3) Regarding the color of the underpainting, always select colors that will, in some manner, enhance the final colors. For example, when pink or

a light yellowish color is used under a sky that is eventually to appear blue, and the final blue color is used thinly, the underlying color will influence the blue, making it luminous and radiant. If we choose a green for the underpainting of a red object, our sensitivity to red will be materially intensified because we gain a better feel for the red when working over its complimentary color. And when some of the underlying green remains in evidence (that is, not entirely covered by the red) the value of the red will be enrichd by contrast. When glazes are planned, an appropriate color of a light hue must be chosen for the underpainting. In case a final color cannot be visualized in advance, a neutral color should be chosen. As we already know, every pale pastel-like shade— gray, yellowish, pink, greenish—is called "neutral."

(4) The total appearance of an underpainting, illustrated in Figs. 17A and 19A, can be considered as an understatement. It should be predominantly light in color and not defined. The contours of objects should not meet at a hard edge but should be blurred, that is, thoroughly blended because the final appearance of contours cannot be decided in advance. If these contours are blended in the underpainting, blending in final painting becomes easy. Hard contours can be established easily whenever desired.

(5) Here is a recap of important points. The underpainting must be thoroughly dry before painting over it. Therefore it is advisable to use fast drying colors, the most effective of which is umber; even a small addition of umber will make colors mixed with it dry rapidly. Other fast drying colors are Prussian blue and burnt siena.

Before starting the final painting **always rub painting medium over the surface to be overpainted. As I pointed out before, this is not necessary** between **underpaintings because the conditions required for final painting—ease of brushability and fusing— are not important in the underpainting stage.**

Painting a Still Life Step-By-Step
Figs. 17, A, B. As an example I have chosen a composition of simple objects that will demonstrate the gist of the entire procedure just described. These objects were selected not for "artistic" reasons but merely to illustrate a logical utilization of underpainting.

Step 1. Fig. 17A. The underpainting. The first object—the basket—was underpainted with yellow ochre, white, and some umber. This should be considered a "middle tone," for it is darker than the light tones as they appear on the objects, but lighter than the shadows. The apples in the basket were underpainted in green—umber and cadmium yellow.

The second object, the bottle, was underpainted in the color of its highlights, that is, a light gray—umber and white.

The third object, the mortar, because it is white in color, was underpainted in a dark color— umber, Prussian blue, and some white. The reason for this is that white, in most instances, is used more thickly than any other color; therefore a dark tone under the white will require us to use either a stronger impasto or employ a scumble of a lighter color over the dark color.

As to the background color, as a rule, it is impossible to previsualize it definitely. The definite color as well as its values—light or dark—can only be correctly established when the main motifs are finished, or almost finished. The background, of course, is a mere foil for the motifs and should serve to enhance the objects of the composition. Therefore we underpaint our backgrounds in neutral colors. In our example I have chosen a pink—Venetian red and white—and for the narrow strip of the

wall at the right, ochre and white. For the table top, umber, ochre, and white; and for the piece of paper under the basket, Prussian blue, umber, and white.

Step 2, Fig. 17B. The overpainting. The dry underpainting was moistened with the medium, then the basket was glazed with umber—all of it, the wicker and the empty spaces in between.

Step 3. Next, ochre mixed with white was scumbled with the painting knife into the wet glaze in the areas of the light.

Step 4. The dark areas were strengthened with umber, using a striper and script liner for linear definitions.

Step 5. The green color of the underpainting in the area of the apples was left untouched for the shadows. Venetian red was used for the light areas; Prussian blue and Venetian red for the darkest accents.

Step 6. The bottle was glazed with burnt siena and viridian green. Highlights were produced by wiping the glaze off with a cheesecloth, revealing the light underpainting.

Step 7. The mortar received heavy overpaint of white with occasional dabs of red to liven up the stark white. In the shadows, Prussian blue, white, and umber were brushed in with a bristle brush.

Step 8. For the background, painted entirely with the painting knife, Prussian blue, white, umber, and ochre were used. The shadow on the wall at the right side was glazed with Prussian blue and umber; the yellow underpainting of the upper part of this area was allowed to remain unchanged. The color of the table top was glazed with umber into which ochre mixed with umber was scumbled with the painting knife. For the shadows cast by the objects, ultramarine was added to the umber-ochre color.

Step 9. Finally, a script liner was used to enliven the texture of the table surface by suggesting the grain of wood.

In the example above practically the entire range of techniques, with the exception of excessive impasti, was brought into play, and all the tools at our disposal were employed. Because umber, burnt siena, and Prussian blue—the quick drying colors—were used, the painting dried in one day.

As soon as the paint within the impasto also appears dry (thicker applications require considerably longer drying time), corrective overpainting can be done if needed. Overpainting is done always on a surface moistened by the medium. Rough impasti, should be sandpapered before overpainting in order to avoid unpleasant textural effects. To prevent trickling of paint, see page 23, turpentine should be brushed over the surface before overpainting.

Figure 18A.
Schematic representation of
light and shade patterns
In the examples here, the
area of shade prevails

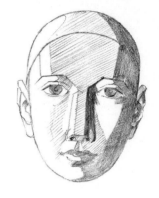

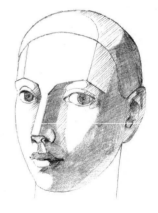

Half shadows

Deepest shadows

Figure 18B.
Schematic representation
of light and shade patterns
In the examples here, the
area of light prevails

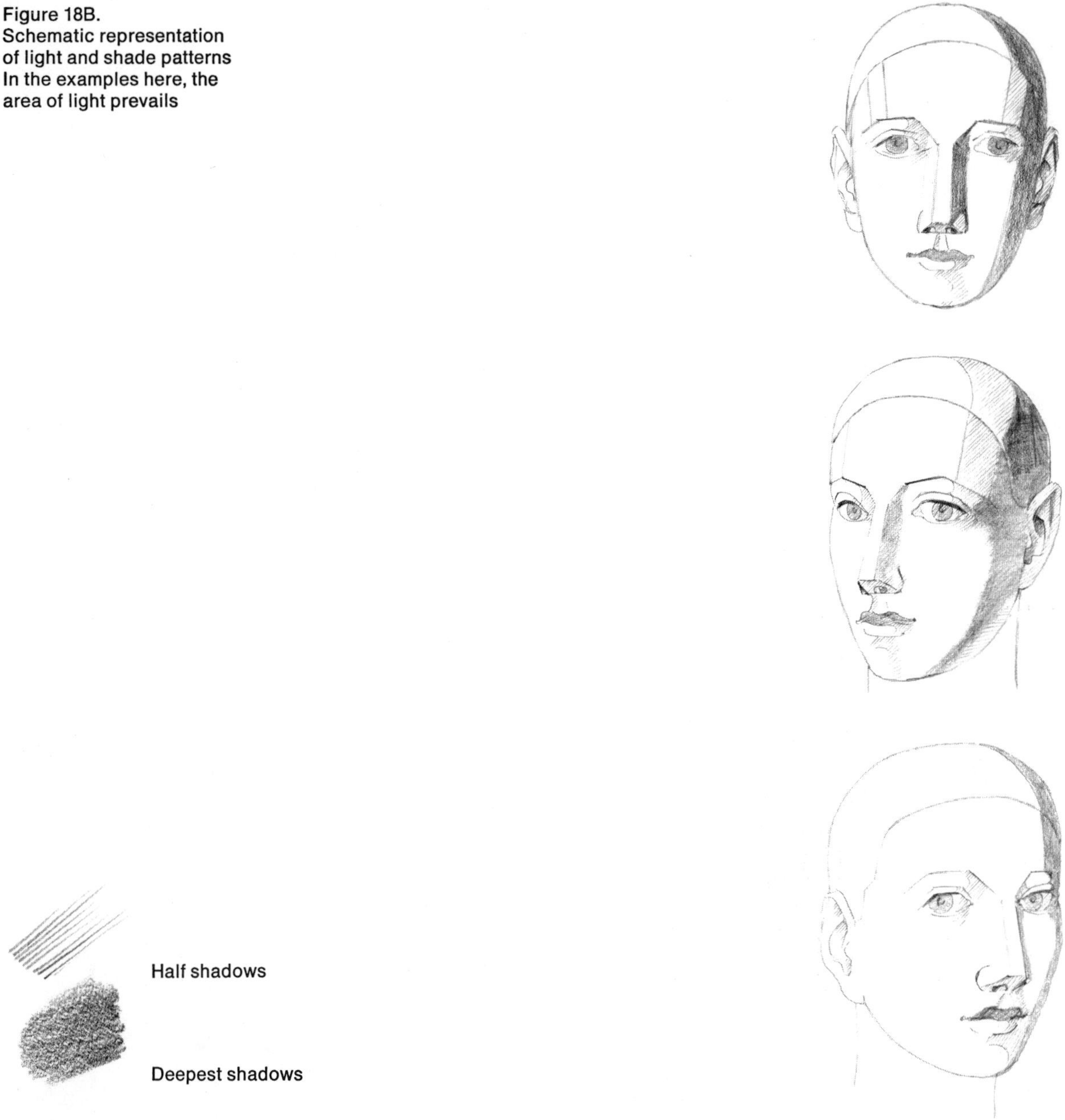

Half shadows

Deepest shadows

Figure 19.
A Portrait in Grisaille
Technique

A. Grisaille

B. Grisaille covered by a glaze

C. Shadows painted into the glaze

Painting a Portrait Step-By-Step

Figs. 18 A, B demonstrate lighting a portrait. Figs. 19, A, B, C, D, show four stages of portrait painting using the classical grisaille technique. Canvas carrying a toned ground is best for this technique. The tone will facilitate progress; a white ground would impede it.

Lighting A Portrait

First of all, before starting to paint a portrait, its proper lighting must be considered. Figs. 18A, B, show three principle positions of the head and the manner of lighting. In this regard, experience teaches us that it is more advantageous for the subject—and also easier for the painter— to have the area of light outweigh the area of shade. Furthermore, if the head is turned toward the light (not away from it), the problems that one usually encounters in portrait painting become less complex.

Grisaille Technique

Grisaille simply means painting in gray colors only, using grays of any desirable kind. These grays should always be light, to give the impression of an "understatement." Light gray, greenish gray, or brownish gray are the most satisfactory tones for the purpose. The recommended tones are prepared from (1) umber and white, (2) umber, Prussian blue, and white, (3) umber, ochre, Prussian blue, and white. The value of the toned ground should be more or less like that in Fig. 19, A. Tone should be applied to the canvas thinly with a painting knife. The paint should be forced into the interstices of the fabric and all surplus paint should be scraped off. In our example the toned ground was made of umber and white. After the ground was dry, we followed our usual procedure—drawing in outlines only and spraying with fixative.

Step 1, Fig. 19, A. The Grisaille. The head was modeled in terms of light and shade using the grisaille method. Observe that in the example, details are lacking, the light areas appear fairly dim, and the shadows are kept in a lighter hue than actually seen. The grisaille was carried out entirely with the short bristle brushes and a rather stiff paint: umber, Prussian blue, and white. Blending was done with painting knife Number 2.

Figure 19D.
Finished Portrait in
Grisaille Technique

After this, the drawing of the features was strengthened, using the round sable brush Number 2 and umber color. The area of the turban was underpainted in pink because a blue was planned as the final color. As can be seen in the illustration, this surface shows very scanty modeling. The background as well as the dress remained untouched. Here we see the original color of the toned ground.

Now, when the first grisaille is dry but the likeness has not yet been sufficiently established, a second and third grisaille can be painted on top of it in neutral colors but in more detail. Even in the last grisaille painting, eyes and lips should not have their final color; they should continue to appear as an understatement, painted in a weaker tint. Oiling between the underpaintings is unnecessary.

Step 2, Fig. 19, B. Painting over the grisaille. A "middle tone" was spread over the entire oiled grisaille. The middle tone is a color darker than the light tones, but lighter than the tone of the shadows. Here this was mixed from ochre, light red, ultramarine, umber, and white, and kept thin to act as a glaze.

Step 3, Fig. 19, C. Here painting was done into the wet flesh-color glaze. The shadows were strengthened, using umber, light red, ochre, ultramarine and white.

Step 4. Next, the drawing of the features was completed with a round sable brush.

Step 5. Finishing the painting. The light tones—
ochre mixed with white—were brushed onto the proper areas opaquely and blended with the shadows, using a bristle brush.

Step 6. The hair was painted in glazes—burnt siena mixed with black. Highlights were produced by wiping off the burnt siena glaze, to reveal the light underpainting.

Step 7. The turban was painted with umber, ultramarine blue, and white, using first a bristle brush, then the painting knife Number 2.

Step 8. The striper was used for the linear definition.

Step 9, Fig. 19 D. Lastly, the background and the dress were painted. For the background, black, ochre, and white were used; for the dress the same color, but lighter, was used, applied more thinly. Into this thin (wet) color cadmium red was brushed, leaving much of the original green color showing.

The technique described in these nine steps approximates very closely the technique used by Gainsborough.

Should your painting require corrections after the final step, they can be made in this way: When the painting is dry, in a few days, it can be oiled, and then repainted as desired. It is important to observe the following **rule:** When painting a lighter flesh color onto a darker dry color, the original darker tone should first be brushed in thinly, and the lighter color painted into the wet darker tone. **This will prevent unpleasant "patchy" effects when repainting flesh color.**

Here is a brief summary of the painting procedure I have just described.
For the toned ground and underpainting of flesh—umber, Prussian blue,

white; for underpainting the turban—light red, and white. In the final painting: for flesh—umber, light red, ochre, ultramarine, white; for the turban—Prussian blue, umber, white; for the hair—burnt siena, black; for the background—black, ochre, white; for the dress—cadmium red. The following tools were used: the three painting knives, all our round sable brushes, and two bristle brushes.

How to Paint Hair

At this point we shall discuss painting hair which, because of its particular texture, can be done entirely in glazes. Glazes, as we now know, are always transparent or semi-transparent applications, and "true" glazes are simply a darker color without white considerably thinned by the medium. (However, the exception to this general rule is when painting flesh; here white must be used even when painting shadows transparently.) When painting hair, the light underpainting is glazed with the specific color of the hair without admixture of white. For example, let us assume that the hair is red. In this case the underpainting will be ochre and white. A glaze of burnt siena on top will produce a glowing red color, and an addition of black will strengthen it in the shadow area; wiping the wet top color off will reveal the underpainting and thus provide us with the highlights. This makes it clear that the hair was underpainted in the color of the highlights.

For black hair, of bluish cast, for example, the entire underpainting is done in a light bluish tone, and ultramarine and umber, which together produce a deep black, is glazed over it. Again, wiping off the dark color in places that appear highlighted will free the light underpainting to serve as the needed highlights. This description demonstrates that the working method is not different from the one described in painting the apple and the bottle in Figs. 13 and 17. In fact, when using classical techniques, we are always facing identical principles regardless of the subject matter.

Painting Landscapes: General Procedure

Our general procedure for painting landscapes will be the same for all landscape motifs, whatever their nature. No different or more complex technique will be called for regardless of the scene we choose to paint.

Landscape painting in alla prima on imprimatura was described in Chapter 8. In what way does landscape developed on an underpainting differ from one painted alla prima? Firstly, we are concerned here with canvas which, in contrast to the rigid panel, allows the free use of the painting knife and also offers greater possibilities for developing textures. Moreover, on a canvas overpainting can be carried out more easily. The alla prima method, on the other hand, does not allow overpainting to any extent because this would cover the imprimatura and the painting would then lose its freshness and transparency. Furthermore, alla prima work is limited in size. But a canvas support can be used advantageously in any size. To sum up, for small sketchy work, the alla prima technique is a good choice. For a more elaborate procedure that will permit slow and well-considered progress, the underpainting technique on canvas is more appropriate. The technique described below applies to any landscape you want to paint.

Underpainting and Overpainting Landscapes

The Sky. **Our color choice for underpainting a sky can be either a light pink (Venetian red and white), light yellow (ochre and white), or a gray (Prussian blue, umber, and white).**

For the final colors, a blue for the color of the sky can be mixed either from Prussian blue, umber, and white, or from ultramarine, umber, and white. In the first mixture the prevailing tonality will be greenish, in the second it will be purplish.

Gray skies of almost any tonality can be easily achieved. As we know, viridian green and white with umber, or with Venetian red, and cadmium red will produce a variety of grays. All these can be intermixed for painting gray skys. For darker clouds, a useful combination of colors is

ultramarine and burnt siena.

The only yellow that can be used for atmospheric effects is Naples, for this color, unlike the cadmiums, does not have the tendency to advance toward the foreground when it is placed in the background. Ochre mixed with white is also a pale yellow, but its tonality is warm and "earthy." If one wishes to use a color range such as is found in some flamboyant sunsets, alizarin crimson, cadmium yellow, and red, and other strong colors will have to be considered.

The Greens. **These include trees, meadows, plants. Everything verdant should be underpainted in a yellow color, because when green colors are painted thinly over yellow they will lend life to the final color. In other words, the yellow should be there when called upon. The intensity of the yellow should depend on the key of the final color of the object and, most importantly, on its location in space. That is, the closer the object is to the foreground, the stronger the color of the underpainting can be. In the middle distance the underpainting should be kept in a low key; cadmium yellow would be inappropriate but light ochre mixed with white will do well. In the distant background the yellows will disappear altogether. Here a light gray will be the suitable color for underpainting of all motifs such as forests, mountains, and plains.**

When using green colors one should remember that the liveliest green will be obtained from mixtures of cadmium yellow and viridian green or ultramarine. If blues predominate, the green will appear more distant. The more white enters the mixture, the grayer, hence still more distant, the general tone becomes. The strongest greens result from a combination of either Prussian blue, umber or black, with cadmium yellow. For the darkest transparent greens, burnt siena and Prussian blue (without white) should be used; when painted thinly over yellow, these greens will have great depth and luminosity. We should also remember that glazing viridian green or black as well as any one of our blues over a yellow underpainting will produce radiant greens.

Water. **Whether it is a sea, lake, or stream, gray is the best color for underpainting water regardless of its final color. A suitable gray will be**

produced from Prussian blue, umber, and white, mixed to a hue
approximating the toned ground used in portrait painting, see **Fig. 19.**

Regarding the final color of water, the best advice I can give the student
is this—do not go overboard on blue because nothing will conjure up
the impression of a calendar picture more quickly than water painted in
"Capri Grotto" blue color. Keep the following range of color mixtures in
mind—they will be on the greenish rather than the bluish side—viridian
and white; ochre, black, and white; ochre, viridian, and white; ochre,
viridian, black, and white. A small amount of Prussian blue can be added
to every suggested mixture, for bluish tints.

Chapter 10.

The Use of Various Technical Devices

Fig. 20, The Rock, our last picture, combines every possible technical device. That is why I selected this as an all-inclusive example of painting a landscape. As a matter of fact, this picture was painted as a demonstration in one of my classes, in three sessions of less than one hour each. Here is the method I used:

The Rock Step-By-Step

The first underpainting was done exclusively with a painting knife. The area of the sky was covered with light pink, mixed from Venetian red and white. The rock was underpainted in umber, Prussian blue, and white in a rather dark tone, in the areas of the light; but the entire area of the shadow was covered by ochre and white, which reversed the actual appearance of these areas.

The green foreground was underpainted with cadmium yellow and white. No medium was used, and a trace of umber—small enough not to influence the color to any degree—was added to all the colors employed which greatly accelerated their drying. Two days later the underpainting was dry enough for overpaints. This was done only in the area of the rock for the purpose of strengthening its texture. Here a bristle brush was used to make this texture more perceptible. The color of the second underpainting remained unchanged, quite dark for light parts, and light for the part in the shadow. However, the surface of the area in the shadow was kept rather smooth, whereas strong rough impasto covered the side of the rock turned toward the light. This completed the underpainting. Then, two days later, when the underpainting has dried sufficiently, the entire painting, measuring 16 by 20 inches, was executed in the following manner:

Step 1. The surface was oiled with Copal Painting Medium.

Step 2. The sky. Prussian blue, umber, and white were brushed in roughly with a bristle brush and smoothed with painting knife Number 2. The white clouds were brushed in with the large round sable brush, the white color greatly diluted by the medium.

Step 3. The entire area of the rock was glazed with umber and Prussian blue, which did not register much on the dark area but created a beautiful, luminous transparence in the shadows.

Step 4. The light part of the rock was given a heavy overpaint of white and ochre, with painting knife Number 3. The knife, gliding over the top of the rough impasto of the underpainting, left many spots uncovered. Because these spots remained dark, they suggest crevices in the rock. On the dark side, the stratification of the rock mass was indicated with a script liner.

Step 5. Finally, in the foreground, the greens—mixed from Prussian blue and cadmium yellow, and from umber and cadmium yellow—were painted with the painting knife. Details were put in with a script liner and a striper.

For the entire painting, only the following six colors were used: white, Venetian red, ochre, cadmium yellow, umber, and Prussian blue. In addition to all our painting knives, one script liner, the striper, the largest round sable brush, and two bristle brushes, Number 8 and 10, were used. However, the painting shows mainly the evidence of palette knife work and the work of the round soft hair brushes; bristle brush marks appear only on isolated spots of the rock.

The Rock has the following marked characteristics: a heavy impasto in the light areas, a relatively smooth appearance in the shadows; all the green, the large masses as well as the smaller details, show considerable impasto which can be seen in the photographs of details, Figs. 21, A, B, C. These photographs also reveal the impasto textures characteristic of paint that has an addition of Copal Concentrate. The impasti are high and smooth-edged; in their conformation they resemble those seen in the work of the early Flemish and Italian masters.

Figure 20.
The Rock.
A painting using various
technical devices

Figure 21A.
Detail from Figure 20

Figure 21B.
Detail from Figure 20

Figure 21C.
Detail from Figure 20

Chapter 11.

Varnishing Paintings

Unlike alla prima paintings where the single application of paint, conditioned by Copal Concentrate (especially important when painting alla prima), dries with perfect gloss and does not require varnishing, paintings on an underpainting must be varnished. This is because the colors will "sink in," and as they become flat they lose their depth and often even their identity. The smaller the amount of the medium that was intermixed with the color, the duller the color will appear. Dullness also results from the absorption of oil by the underlying strata of paint which remains porous for a long time.

Varnishing, therefore, needs to be done, first to revive the colors, and second to protect the painting from atmospheric dirt that will settle on its surface. In time the dirt may incorporate itself into the paint film and obscure its original appearance. To prevent this from happening, as soon as a painting is superficially dry, that is, in about two to four weeks, it should be varnished with Retouching Varnish.

Our long bristle brush, or a small utility brush can be used for varnishing. The varnish should be applied thinly without much pressure on the brush, for the surface of a freshly dried painting is very vulnerable. Varnishing a painting at least one year old can be done by means of a piece of cheesecloth. Cheesecloth is very useful for this purpose because it distributes the varnish evenly and sparingly—in fact, during this process the painting also receives a cleaning.

Retouching Varnish will not last well on freshly dried surfaces; within six months or a year the painting will have to be revarnished. Sometimes even after revarnishing dull spots will reappear, but in this case (if a painting is a year old or older), Damar Picture Varnish should be used. This "final" varnish will remain on the surface of a thoroughly dry painting for many years. In my experience, Permanent Pigments Copal Varnish has also proved to be completely suitable as a final varnish because it is not too glossy and it possesses unexcelled durability.

Sometimes a painting may call for a mat surface. A mat surface is especially desirable for murals and similar large decorative paintings, or where lighting conditions in a room would make a glossy painting surface reflect light. Such reflections can be most disturbing. They may block out the view of part of a painting or even of the entire painting. It is advisable in such circumstances to use a varnish that largely eliminates gloss. Matte Picture Varnish produced according to my formula is such a varnish.

The varnish applied to a paint surface may not always spread evenly; it may "trickle," as happens when oiling before underpainting. There is no ready explanation for this. However, trickling can be prevented by rubbing the varnish-moistened surface with the side of one's hand—but only a thoroughly dry surface can be treated in this manner, for relatively fresh paint films, glazes in particular, are quite vulnerable.

Not infrequently, even after varnishing with Damar Picture Varnish, dull spots may reappear and they may remain dull even after repeated varnishing. Certain earth pigments may account for this, or the dull appearance of these spots may be due to a loss of the pigment's vehicle; a crack in the priming of the canvas sometimes drains the vehicle or the medium. Should this occur, the dull spots should be treated with the Copal Painting Medium. It is best to apply the medium with one's finger and rub it firmly into the affected areas.

Glossary

Alla prima. Painting from start to finish, wet in wet, in one operation.

Chiaroscuro. Interrelation of light and dark effects.

Gel. A jelly-like substance.

Gesso. Italian for gypsum. Designates an aqueous priming material (usually white) bound by a size or a synthetic material.

Glaze. A transparent film of a darker color applied to a light underpainting.

Grisaille. Underpainting in gray colors.

Gum (turpentine, damar, etc.). Exudates from certain coniferous trees.

Hiding power. The degree of opacity in paint.

Impasto. A thick application of paint.

Imprimatura. Paint thinned by varnish to watercolor consistency applied to the white panel or canvas before painting.

Long paint. Paint that has the tendency to level off, and form soft-edged configurations.

Pastose. Paint applied thickly.

Pigment. The term refers to dry color only.

Relining. Mounting a painting on a new canvas.

Resin, Hard. Fossil exudates of certain coniferous trees now extinct.

Resin, soft. Exudates from some living coniferous trees.

Scumble. A semi-opaque application of a light color on a dark underpainting.

Short paint. Paint that retains its hard configuration when applied with a brush or palette knife.

Siccative (dryer). Metallic salts used for speeding up the drying process of oils.

Size. An aqueous solution of glue or gelatine.

Stand oil. Linseed oil cooked at high temperatures in the absence of air.

Stabilizers. Materials used to keep the pigment and oil in suspension when stored in tubes or cans.

Tooth. The grainy or rough quality of a surface.

Varnish. A solution of a resin in a volatile diluent.